AMSTERDAM

teNeues

AMSTERDAM

Photographs by Bonnie Josephson
Text by Micki O'Flynn

teNeues

Amsterdam offers her admirers a feast for sore eyes. Imagine the challenge of grasping its richness in only two colors. Just as there are many ways to describe in a single language those Dutch gray skies (steely, woolly, cloudy, overcast, foggy, to name a few), this photo collection in black-and-white vividly illustrates the contrasts found in this brilliant city.

Amsterdam's mix of contemporary and classic, permissive and punctual, art and commerce, race and culture creates an atmosphere as many-faceted as the diamonds it trades.

There is **physical Amsterdam**: open *pleins* (squares) ringed with shops and cafés; boats and bicycles, trams and taxis, busy with the business of people on the move; everywhere, pedestrians hustling under umbrellas; streets spreading like a web over a network of waterways. Because of this, Amsterdam is a place of bridges.

There is **clichéd Amsterdam**: tulips and wooden shoes for sale in the tourist shops; marijuana menus on display in coffee shops.

There is **historic Amsterdam**: the spirits of Rembrandt, Vermeer, and Anne Frank are revered. The glorious days of the Golden Age are recalled in the mansions along the canals. World-class museums beckon with outstanding collections from Van Gogh, the Dutch Masters, and more. The losses of World War II and the German occupation are remembered in memorials around town.

There is **sensuous Amsterdam**: the rich perfume from exotic flowers at the *Bloemmarkt* (flower market); the froth on your lips from an icy mug of Dutch beer; the sound of raindrops on your jacket; the smell of herring for sale on the sidewalk.

There is **everyday Amsterdam**: pay attention to the tinkling of those bells. A mother carrying her three children on a bicycle—as well as her groceries—approaches from behind. The Albert Cuyp Market overflows with residents rooting for bargains in vendors' stalls. Sidewalk cafes are full of locals enjoying their *koffietijd* (coffee break) and reading their morning *krant* (newspaper). East meets west in a young couple's kiss.

Amsterdam is a place that allows differences to flourish. With its live-and-let-live attitude, life here is a non-competitive sport. Like Dutch grammar, its people can be direct; yet like the images of Amsterdam, they possess depths of contrast, diversity and beauty.

Micki O'Flynn

Amsterdam bietet seinen Bewunderern ein Fest für die Augen. Man stelle sich die Herausforderung vor, dem Reichtum der Stadt mit nur zwei Farben gerecht zu werden. Gerade weil es in einer einzigen Sprache schon so viele Möglichkeiten gibt, diesen grauen (stählernen, wolligen, wolkigen, bedeckten, nebligen, um nur einiges zu nennen) holländischen Himmel zu beschreiben, illustriert die vorliegende Fotokollektion in Schwarzweiß lebendig die Kontraste dieser brillanten Stadt.

Amsterdams Mischung aus Gegenwärtigem und Klassischem, Freizügigkeit und Genauigkeit, Kunst und Kommerz, ethnischer Herkunft und Kultur erschafft eine Atmosphäre, die so viele Facetten hat wie die Diamanten, mit denen hier gehandelt wird.

Es gibt das **physische Amsterdam**: offene *Pleins* (Plätze) umgeben von Läden und Cafés; Boote und Fahrräder, Straßenbahnen und Taxis, deren Geschäft es ist, geschäftige Menschen zu transportieren; überall drängen sich Fußgänger unter Schirmen; ein Gewirr von Straßen breitet sich über ein Netz von Wasserwegen. Deshalb ist Amsterdam ein Ort der Brücken.

Es gibt das **klischeehafte Amsterdam**: Tulpen und Holzschuhe stehen zum Verkauf in Touristenläden; Marihuana-Karten liegen in Coffeeshops aus.

Es gibt das **historische Amsterdam**: Der Geist von Rembrandt, Vermeer und Anne Frank werden geehrt. Die glanzvollen Tage des Goldenen Zeitalters werden heraufbeschworen von den herrschaftlichen Häusern entlang der Kanäle. Museen von Weltklasse locken mit herausragenden Sammlungen von Van Gogh, den Niederländischen Meistern und anderen. An die Verluste des Zweiten Weltkriegs und die deutsche Besatzung wird in der ganzen Stadt mit Gedenkstätten erinnert.

Es gibt das **sinnliche Amsterdam**: der intensive Duft exotischer Blüten am *Bloemmarkt* (Blumenmarkt); der Schaum von eiskaltem holländischen Bier auf den Lippen; das Platschen der Regentropfen auf deiner Jacke; der Geruch von Hering, der auf dem Bürgersteig verkauft wird.

Es gibt das **alltägliche Amsterdam**: Achte auf das Klingeln. Von hinten nähert sich eine Mutter mit drei Kindern auf dem Fahrrad – ihre Einkäufe hat sie ebenfalls dabei. Der Albert-Cuyp-Markt quillt über von Bewohnern, die an den Marktständen nach Angeboten suchen. Die Straßencafés sind voll von Einheimischen, die ihre *Koffietijd* (Kaffeepause) genießen und ihre *Krant* (Zeitung) lesen. Ost und West treffen sich im Kuss eines jungen Paares.

Amsterdam ist ein Ort, der Unterschieden zu gedeihen erlaubt. Leben und leben lassen ist hier die Grundhaltung, und das Leben ist selbst ein Sport ohne Konkurrenz. So direkt wie die holländische Grammatik sind die Menschen hier; wie die Bilder von Amsterdam besitzen sie Tiefe im Kontrast, Vielfalt und Schönheit.

Micki O'Flynn

Amsterdam offre à ses admirateurs une fête de couleurs pour les yeux. C'est donc un défi de vouloir saisir la richesse de cette ville en deux couleurs seulement. De même qu'il y a de nombreuses manières de décrire dans une langue les ciels gris de Hollande (ciel d'acier, laineux, nuageux, couvert, brumeux, pour n'en nommer que quelques-unes), de même cette collection de photos en noir et blanc illustre de manière vivante les contrastes de cette ville extraordinaire.

Amsterdam est un mélange d'éléments contemporain et classique, permissif et rigoureux, artistique et commercial, ethnique et culturel créant une atmosphère variée avec autant de facettes que les diamants dont la ville pratique le négoce.

Il y a l'**Amsterdam physique** : des *pleins* (places) ouverts, entourés de magasins et de cafés, des bateaux et des bicyclettes, des trams et des taxis occupés à transporter ceux qui s'affairent, des piétons pressés sous leurs parapluies, des rues recouvrant comme une toile le réseau de voies d'eau. Ainsi les ponts sont nombreux dans la ville.

Il y a l'**Amsterdam des clichés** : des tulipes et des chaussures en bois vendues dans les magasins pour touristes, des coffee shops proposant de la marijuana au menu.

Il y a l'**Amsterdam historique** : l'esprit de Rembrandt, de Vermeer et d'Anne Frank est toujours vénéré. Les demeures le long des canaux évoquent les jours glorieux de l'âge d'or. Avec des collections exceptionnelles de Van Gogh, des grands maîtres hollandais et d'autres, les musées jouissent d'une réputation international et attirent des visiteurs du monde entier. Des monuments rappellent un peu partout dans la ville les pertes de la Seconde Guerre mondiale et l'occupation allemande.

Il y a l'**Amsterdam sensuelle** : le parfum intensif des fleurs exotiques du *Bloemmarkt* (marché aux fleurs), la mousse sur vos lèvres après une chope de bière hollandaise glacée, le bruit des gouttes de pluie sur votre veste, l'odeur du hareng que l'on vend sur le trottoir.

Il y a l'**Amsterdam de tous les jours** : attention au tintement de sonnette. Derrière vous, une mère à vélo, avec ses trois enfants et ses achats, vous avertit de son passage. Le marché Albert Cuyp grouille d'acheteurs à la recherche d'aubaines. Les terrasses de café sont occupées par les gens du quartier qui font leur *koffietijd* (pause-café) en lisant leur *krant* (journal). L'Est et l'Ouest se rencontrent dans le baiser d'un jeune couple.

Amsterdam est un lieu qui tolère la différence en ayant pour devise, vivre et laisser vivre. La vie est ici un sport sans concurrence. Comme la grammaire néerlandaise, les habitants d'Amsterdam peuvent être directs, et comme les photos d'Amsterdam, leurs contrastes, leurs différences et leur beauté sont multiples.

Micki O'Flynn

Amsterdam ofrece a sus admiradores un festival para los ojos. Imagínese el desafío de hacer justicia a la riqueza de la ciudad con sólo dos colores. Precisamente porque en un solo idioma ya existen tantas posibilidades de describir este gris cielo holandés (férreo, lanoso, nublado, cubierto, nebuloso, por citar unas pocas), la presente colección de fotografías en blanco y negro ilustra vivamente los contrastes de esta brillante ciudad.

La mezcla en Amsterdam de lo contemporáneo y lo clásico, la permisividad y la precisión, el arte y el comercio, las etnias y las culturas crea una atmósfera que tiene tantas facetas como los diamantes con los que aquí se comercia.

Existe el **Amsterdam físico**: *Pleins* (plazas) abiertos rodeados de tiendas y cafés; embarcaciones y bicicletas, tranvías y taxis, cuyo negocio es el de transportar a personas ajetreadas; Por todas partes se agolpan peatones debajo de paraguas; Las calles se despliegan como una tela sobre una red de vías navegables. Por eso, Amsterdam es un lugar de puentes.

Existe el **Amsterdam de los clichés**: Los tulipanes y los zuecos están a la venta en las tiendas para turistas. Los menús de marihuana están expuestos en los Coffee Shops.

Existe el **Amsterdam histórico**: Los espíritus de Rembrandt, Vermeer y Ana Frank son venerados. Las casas señoriales a lo largo de los canales evocan los gloriosos días de la Época Dorada. Los museos de clase mundial atraen con colecciones excepcionales de Van Gogh, de los maestros holandeses y de otros. Por toda la ciudad en lugares conmemorativos se recuerdan las pérdidas de la Segunda Guerra Mundial y la ocupación alemana.

Existe el **Amsterdam sensual**: el aroma intenso de las flores exóticas en el *Bloemmarkt* (mercado de flores); la espuma de una helada jarra de cerveza holandesa en sus labios; el chapoteo de las gotas de lluvia en su chaqueta; el olor del arenque que se vende en la calle.

Existe el **Amsterdam cotidiano**: Fíjese en el sonar de los timbres. Una madre llevando a sus tres hijos – y también sus compras – en la bicicleta se acerca desde atrás. El mercado Albert Cuyp rebosa de habitantes buscando gangas en los puestos. Las terrazas de los cafés están llenas de lugareños disfrutando de su *Koffietijd* (pausa para el café) y leyendo su *Krant* (periódico) de la mañana. El este y el oeste se encuentran en el beso de una pareja joven.

Amsterdam es un lugar que permite que las diferencias florezcan. Vivir y dejar vivir es aquí la actitud y la vida misma es un deporte sin competencia. Las personas son aquí tan directas como la gramática holandesa. Pero como las imágenes de Amsterdam, poseen profundidad de contraste, variedad y belleza.

Micki O'Flynn

Amsterdam offre ai suoi ammiratori una festa per gli occhi. Immaginatevi allora la sfida a cui ci si trova davanti volendo catturare la ricchezza di questa città con due soli colori. Proprio perché già in una sola lingua ci sono così tante possibilità di descrivere questi cieli grigi (plumbei, foschi, nuvolosi, coperti, nebbiosi, per citarne solo alcune), la presente raccolta di fotografie in bianco e nero illustra vividamente i contrasti di questa brillante città.

Il mix di contemporaneità e classicità, permissività e precisione, arte e commercio, provenienze e culture crea un'atmosfera dalle numerose sfaccettature, come i diamanti di cui qui fiorisce il commercio.

C'è l'**Amsterdam fisica**: gli ampi *plein* (piazze) su cui si affacciano negozi e caffè; barche e biciclette, tram e taxi, il cui compito è trasportare persone indaffarate; ovunque i pedoni vanno di fretta, con i loro ombrelli; un groviglio di strade si posa su una rete di canali. Per questo Amsterdam è una città di ponti.

C'è l'**Amsterdam dei cliché**: tulipani e zoccoli di legno in vendita nei negozi di souvenir; menù di marijuana nei coffeeshop.

C'è l'**Amsterdam storica**: si rende onore allo spirito di Rembrandt, Vermeer e Anna Frank. I palazzi lungo i canali rievocano i giorni gloriosi dell'età d'oro. Musei di fama mondiale attirano visitatori con eccezionali collezioni di Van Gogh, della scuola fiamminga e di altri artisti. In tutta la città i monumenti commemorativi ricordano le perdite della seconda guerra mondiale e l'occupazione tedesca.

C'è l'**Amsterdam dei sensi**: l'intenso profumo dei fiori esotici al *Bloemmarkt* (il mercato dei fiori); la schiuma di un boccale di birra olandese ben fredda sulle labbra; il ticchettio delle gocce di pioggia sulla giacca; l'odore delle aringhe in vendita sui marciapiedi.

C'è l'**Amsterdam quotidiana**: senti il campanello di una bicicletta. Alle tue spalle si avvicina una mamma in bicicletta con tre bambini – e con tutta la spesa. L'Albert Cuyp straripa di persone che rovistano sui banchetti a caccia di occasioni. I caffè all'aperto sono pieni di gente del luogo che si gode il suo *koffietijd* (pausa caffè) leggendo il *krant* (giornale). Est ed ovest si incontrano nel bacio di due giovani.

Amsterdam è un luogo che permette alle differenze di prosperare. Vivere e lasciar vivere: la vita stessa qui è uno sport non competitivo. Come la grammatica olandese, la gente non è contorta, e possiede profondità nel contrasto, diversità e bellezza come le immagini di Amsterdam.

Micki O'Flynn

13 ▣

geuzenveld

624

speculaas
grachtenhuis

€ 25.00

5.= SCHO
7.= KLO
10,= LAA
M.U.V DECOR

ANNE FRANK HUIS

head wear
€ 7.50

UNIEK!
ARTIKEL V/H JAAR!
GLASVIJL

Directory   Verzeichnis   Table des matières   Directorio   Indice delle materie

65	Keizersgracht	91	Herengracht
66	Oude Leliestraat, Coffee Shop	92	Lijbaansbrug
67	Oude Leliestraat, Coffee Shop	93	Brouwersgracht
68	Keizersgracht	94	Lindengracht, Jordaan
69	Lijnbaanssteeg, Smart Shop	95	Lindengracht, Jordaan
70	Prinsengracht from Westerkerk	96	Johnny Jordaanplein
71	Herengracht	97	Elandsgracht, Jordaan
	Leliegracht	98	Lijnbaansgracht, Melkweg Club
72	Westerkerk, Prinsengracht	99	Rozengracht
73	Westerkerk, Rozengracht	100	Sarphatipark
74	Anne Frankhuis, Prinsengracht		Café in Vondelpark
75	Anne Frankhuis, Prinsengracht	101	Vondelpark
76/77	Brouwersgracht	102	Vondelpark
78	Herenstraat	103	Vondelpark
79	Prinsengracht		Noordermarkt
80	Lekkeresluis	104/105	Rijksmuseum
	Blauwburgwal	106	Museumplein
81	Keizersgracht	107	Rijksmuseum
	Brouwersgracht	108	Van Gogh Museum
82	Reguliersgracht	109	Concertgebouw, Museumplein
83	Herengracht	110	Albert Cuypstraat Market
	Keizersgracht, Amsterdam Police		Albert Cupystraat Market
84	Herenstraat, Toy Store	111	Albert Cuypstraat Market
85	Prinsenstraat, Santa Jet	112	Albert Cuypstraat Market
86	Oude Leliestraat, Coffee Shop		Lindengracht
87	Lijnbaanssteeg, Smart Shop	113	Albert Cuypstraat Market
	Lijnbaanssteeg, Smart Shop	114	Majanggracht, Java Island
88	Noorderkerk, Prinsengracht	115	De Gooyer Windmill
89	De Krijtberg, Singel	116	Brouwersgracht
90	Leidsegracht	117	Herengracht

Front cover: Prinsengracht from Westerkerk
Back cover: Leliegracht

Photographs © 2004 Bonnie Josephson Photography
© 2004 teNeues Verlag GmbH + Co. KG, Kempen
All rights reserved.

Bonnie Josephson Photography
Postbus 15820
1001 NH Amsterdam - The Netherlands
e-mail: bonnie@bjfoto.com

www.bjfoto.com

Picture and text rights reserved for all countries.
No part of this publication may be reproduced in
any manner whatsoever. All rights reserved.

Photographs by Bonnie Josephson
Design by Iris Durie, Axel Theyhsen
Introduction by Micki O'Flynn
Translation by SWB Communications
Dr. Sabine Werner-Birkenbach (German)
Dominique Le Pluart (French)
Gemma Correa-Buján (Spanisch)
Dr. Nicoletta Negri (Italian)
Editorial coordination by Arndt Jasper
Production by Alwine Krebber
Color separation by Medien Team-Vreden, Germany

While we strive for utmost precision in every detail,
we cannot be held responsible for any inaccuracies,
neither for any subsequent loss or damage arising.

Bibliographic information published by Die Deutsche
Bibliothek. Die Deutsche Bibliothek lists this publication in the Deutsche Nationalbibliographie; detailed
bibliographic data is available in the Internet at
http://dnb.ddb.de

ISBN 3-8238-4577-2

Printed in Italy

Published by teNeues Publishing Group

teNeues Book Division
Kaistraße 18
40221 Düsseldorf
Germany
Phone: 00 49-(0) 2 11-99 45 97-0
Fax: 00 49-(0) 2 11-99 45 97-40
e-mail: books@teneues.de
Press department: arehn@teneues.de
Phone: 00 49-(0) 21 52-916-202

teNeues Publishing Company
16 West 22nd Street
New York, N.Y. 10010
USA
Phone: 001-212-627-9090
Fax: 001-212-627-9511

teNeues Publishing UK Ltd.
P.O. Box 402
West Byfleet
KT14 7ZF
Great Britain
Phone: 0044-1932-403509
Fax: 0044-1932-403514

teNeues France S.A.R.L.
4, rue de Valence
75005 Paris
France
Phone: 00 33-1-55 76 62 05
Fax: 00 33-1-55 76 64 19

www.teneues.com

teNeues Publishing Group
Kempen
Düsseldorf
London
Madrid
New York
Paris

teNeues